Italian Christmas Cookies

And the stories of the Italians
who brought them to New England

By Leslie and Dan Landrigan

Illustrated by Leslie Landrigan

INTRODUCTION

You don't have to be Italian to love Italian Christmas cookies. There are so many varieties and so many different ingredients that you're bound to find at least a few irresistible. Some are even free of gluten and dairy!

But why would the New England Historical Society publish a book about Italian cuisine? That's easy. New England has the densest populations of Italian-Americans in the United States. "Most Italian" honors go back and forth between Connecticut and Rhode Island, and New Haven is the most Italian city in the country. There's plenty of Italian history in New Haven's Wooster Square, Boston's North End and Providence's Federal Hill. There's even more in places you may not realize have large Italian populations.

Food is a fascinating lens through which you can view the history of the Italian people in New England. Each cookie has a story about the past. The ingredients in Sicilian cookies tell of conquests by Greeks, who planted wheat, and by Arabs from North Africa who planted lemon trees. Biscotti started out as shelf-stable sustenance for the Roman legions marching to conquer Britain. The almond paste in pignoli was made by cloistered nuns in Sicilian convents and sold through windows to support the monastery.

These old, old recipes made their way across the Atlantic Ocean, mostly during the Great Migration from 1880 to 1920.

In this book you will get step-by-step instructions on how to make 24 different Italian Christmas cookies in a modern American kitchen. Each recipe comes with a story about the Italian people. You'll read about Italians who came to New England before, during and after the Great Migration. You'll learn some of the history of Christmas and the different regional celebrations that evolved in Italy over the centuries. You'll find out which Italian Christmas cookies don't come from the old country—and which famous Americans have ancestors who did.

Many Italian Christmas cookie recipes in cookbooks and on the Internet accompany nostalgic recollections of the recipe cards that Nonna tucked into a box, the warm smells of cooking and the sound of Frank Sinatra on the hi-fi. This book is not that.

Being Italian in America was more than good food and family visits and delicious treats after Christmas Eve Mass. There was a dark side, too. Italians were shunned, looked down upon, discriminated against. In World War II they were treated as enemy aliens despite the many sons of Italy who fought and died in the conflict. They were stereotyped as criminals, garlic eaters, spaghetti benders, guidos.

But they struggled against hardship and hatred and they prevailed. This book tells of some of those struggles as well as some of the triumphs of the Italian people. And it also gives directions for how to make twenty-four tantalizing Italian Christmas cookies.

Buon Natale!

CONTENTS

1

CHRISTMAS BISCOTTI

TWO POPES AND A HOLIDAY

C hristmas actually started in the Lazian city of Rome. Pope Julius, a Roman who became pope in 337, is said to have decided Christ was born on December 25. (Maybe.) In 590, Gregory the Great, the son of a Roman senator, became pope. He decided the festivals before Christ's birth should evolve into Christian ones, and the Christian festivals should copy the old pagan celebrations. And so in Italy the Saturnalia of the Romans turned into a celebration of Jesus Christ's birth.

Today, the Christmas season begins in Italy on December 8, the Feast of the Immaculate Conception. Decorations go up then: Christmas trees and wreaths, colored lights and nativity scenes, or preseppi, in churches and piazzas. The season ends on January 6, the Feast of the Epiphany.

But that's where the generalization ends. Italians in different regions, and even in different villages within the same region, don't all celebrate Christmas the same way.

Until 1861, Italy was just a collection of independent city states, each with its own traditions, cuisine and identity. Even today, Italy has 139 distinct dialects, and sometimes someone from one region can't understand someone else from another.

So some Italians exchange presents on December 13, the feast of Santa Lucia, the blind saint. Some do it on Christmas Day. Still others hold off until January 6, when the good witch Befana brings children sweets and gifts.

From Rome to Sicily, bagpipers come down from the mountains and serenade the people with folk songs during the eight days before Christmas.

Holiday foods also vary from region to region and village to village. In Calabria and Sicily, people celebrate the feast of Saint Lucia by eating la cuccia, a wheatberry pudding with mosto cotto and ricotta or nuts.

In southern Italy, celebrants eat as many as seven different fish on Christmas Eve, hence the name, the Feast of the Seven Fishes. Many Italians go to midnight Mass, but some northern Italians go skiing by torchlight at midnight. Farther south, they go home and eat caggionetti after midnight Mass.

On Christmas Day, family and friends sit down to a Christmas lunch that defines abbondanza, or abundance. The meal begins with traditional dishes that vary from region to region. Sweets, too, have different shapes, textures and ingredients, depending on where they're from. Sicilians use ricotta, honey, marzipan and pistachios in their desserts. In Campania, they go for lemons, Amarena cherries and ricotta. Calabrians use figs and citrus, while almonds and mosto cotto are typical of Puglia. In Basilicata, they make desserts with walnuts, chestnuts, honey and chickpeas.

Christmas Biscotti

Italians used to refer to all cookies as biscotti. The twice-baked, dunkable cookie has spread throughout Italy and comes in many variations. Here's a Christmas version:

1/2 cup butter

1 cup white sugar

3 large eggs, room temperature

1/2 teaspoon almond extract

2-3/4 cups all-purpose flour

1/2 Tablespoon baking powder

1/4 teaspoon salt

1 cup diced mixed candied fruit

In a bowl, whisk flour, baking powder and salt together. Set aside.

In a large bowl, beat the butter and sugar together until creamy, then beat in the eggs. Stir in almond extract.

Gradually add the flour mixture to the wet ingredients.

Fold in candied fruit by hand.

Refrigerate the dough for an hour.

Preheat oven to 325°.

Divide the dough into 2 equal pieces. If the dough is sticky, wet your hands with cool water to handle more easily.

Cover a baking sheet with parchment paper. Shape each half into a 12-by-2-inch log, place on baking sheet and flatten slightly.

Bake until browned, from 20-25 minutes, depending on your oven. Remove from oven and cool for about 5 minutes.

When the logs are cool enough to handle, cut them into 1-inch thick slices. Put the slices on the baking sheet and toast in the oven for another 10-15 minutes, turning them once to toast each side.

Remove from the oven and cool on a wire rack.

2

Italian Butter Cookies

Perhaps Not What You Think

The use of butter divides northern Italian cooking from the cuisine of central and southern Italy. According to one story, when Julius Caesar visited northern Italy he tasted butter for the first time. It disgusted him.

Southern and central Italians typically used olive oil in cooking, even in sweets. That has changed over time. In the late nineteenth century, Swiss immigrants came to Naples and Palermo, where they introduced butter and cream to baking. Pastry chefs opened fancy bakeries selling elegant treats.

Italians have typically preferred shopping at the pasticceria for elaborate holiday sweets rather than making them at home. They brought that tradition to America, where Italian bakeries still thrive in old Italian neighborhoods.

Many Italian cookie recipes go back to the ancient Greeks and Romans. Butter cookies do not. In fact, the butter cookies you buy in just about any Italian-American bakery are pretty much an American invention.

Italian Butter Cookies

Italian-American butter cookies are fairly easy to make using a pastry bag and the *"frolla montata"* (whipped shortcrust pastry) technique.

1-1/4 cup all-purpose flour

1/2 teaspoon salt

1/2 cup (1 stick) unsalted butter, softened

1/2 cup granulated sugar

1 large egg, room temperature

1 teaspoon vanilla extract

1/2 teaspoon almond flavoring/extract

Optional for toppings: apricot, raspberry or strawberry jam; candied cherries, crumbled pistachios, coconut flakes, whole almonds. Chocolate chips for dipping.

Sift together the flour and salt and set aside.

In a large bowl, combine the butter and sugar. Beat with an electric mixer (or use the whisk attachment with a stand mixer) on medium speed for at least 5 minutes. Mixture should be fluffy.

Add the egg, beating until it is fully absorbed.

Beat in the vanilla and almond extract.

Slowly add the sifted flour until fully incorporated. The dough should be soft and sticky but able to hold its shape.

Transfer the mixture into a clean bowl, cover with plastic and refrigerate for 30 minutes to an hour. (Or you can pipe the cookies onto a baking sheet and then refrigerate them.)

Preheat oven to 350°.

Cover a baking sheet with parchment paper. Transfer the mixture again to a piping bag fitted with a nozzle of your choice and pipe the cookies directly onto the baking sheet. Try S-shaped cookies, logs, flowers or round cookies. Make a well in the center of the round cookies for toppings. Or melt the chocolate chips and dip the cookies into them after they're baked.

If you don't have a pastry bag, just use a tablespoon to scoop the dough and drop it onto the baking sheet.

Bake for 11 to 13 minutes or until golden brown.

Cool for 5 minutes on the baking sheet before transferring the cookies to a wire rack. Store in an airtight container.

3

AMARETTI

FROM RENAISSANCE VENETO TO 20TH-CENTURY NEW HAMPSHIRE

Renaissance Italian cooking, Portsmouth, New Hampshire, and Mary Ann Esposito actually have a few things in common.

The earliest Italian visitors to North America came from Venice, capital of the Veneto region. The Venetian John Cabot—Giovanni Caboto—and his son Sebastian first explored the mainland in North America in 1497 under the commission of English king Henry VII.

During America's colonial era, a smattering of Italian immigrants arrived in New England as missionaries, artisans or political refugees. They tended to be well-educated and well-off.

Early in the eighteenth century, for example, a Venetian named Filippo Traetta got involved in a failed revolution against King Ferdinand IV. He fled the country in 1800 hidden in a merchant vessel owned by the Derby family of Salem, Mass. In 1801 he founded the first music conservatory in Boston as Philip Trajetta.

The Great Migration of Italian immigrants began sometime around 1875 and lasted for fifty years. Four million Italians came to America in the time from 1876 to 1900. They came largely from northern regions, particularly from the mountain areas of Veneto, Friuli, Piedmont and Lombardy.

Amaretti, round cookies made with bitter almonds, originated in Venice during the late Renaissance. Mary Ann Esposito, a student of Renaissance Italian cooking, shared her recipe for them on her cooking show, *Ciao Italia*.

Esposito started her show in 1989 and has been doing it ever since on public television in Durham, New Hampshire. She sometimes cooked on air with her friend Emilio Maddaloni, who ran a one-room lunchroom in nearby Portsmouth for many years.

You may not think of New Hampshire as heavily Italian, but at least ten percent of the population claims some Italian ancestry.

Portsmouth once had a Little Italy, 300 homes in thirty acres for about a thousand people.

Many of Portsmouth's Italians came from the northern Italian region of Romagna, a center of shoe manufacturing. They came to work in Portsmouth's shoe factories and at the shipyard. Many were birds of passage who returned to Italy, but some stayed and moved into the run-down colonial buildings in the North End. Some Italians set up shop as cobblers, barbers and grocers.

By 1920, Portsmouth's Little Italy was 95 percent Italian. It was a crowded waterfront neighborhood with narrow, busy streets and dozens of small businesses, restaurants and shops. Families sold beer and lobster rolls from their homes, popcorn and ice cream from pushcarts. Some people viewed the neighborhood as a slum, with alcohol-fueled fights not uncommon. But Portsmouth's North End slowly acquired middle-class respectability.

Urban renewal in the 1950s and '60s leveled many of the homes, replacing them with a municipal parking lot, the Sheraton Hotel and the old *Portsmouth Herald* building. Only a few of the old buildings survive. But you can still see an Italian presence in Portsmouth at Moe's Italian Sandwiches and the Rosa Restaurant and a number of new Italian eateries.

Amaretti

These delicious treats are both gluten-free and dairy-free.

4 cups blanched whole or slivered almonds

2 cups confectioner's sugar

1 teaspoon double-acting baking powder

4 egg whites at room temperature

Candied cherries

Preheat oven to 375°.

Pulverize almonds into a powder in a food processor. Transfer to a large bowl.

Sift dry ingredients into the almonds.

In a separate bowl, beat egg whites until they form soft peaks.

Fold egg whites into almond mixture, slowly and gently, at first with an up-and-down motion, then with a circular motion, careful not to deflate the egg whites.

Line a baking sheet with parchment paper. Using two spoons, place clumps of the dough onto the parchment. With your thumb, press a hollow into the center of each cookie if you plan to top with cherries. Cut cherries in half and press into the dough. Bake on middle rack of oven for 10-12 minutes. Cool for 5 minutes on baking sheet, then transfer to a wire rack.

4

CRANBERRY PISTACHIO BISCOTTI

YOU SAY BISCOTTI, I SAY CANTUCCI

B iscotti dates to ancient Rome, though it disappeared for a century or two. "Biscotti" comes from the Latin words "bis" for "twice" and "coctum" for "baked," which became "cotto."

Roman cooks baked it once to cook it and twice to dry and preserve it. Because of its long shelf life, it was an ideal food for the Roman legionnaires to take with them while conquering what is now Italy, Greece, Spain and Britain.

Then Rome fell in 110 A.D., and biscotti disappeared from the menu. Then it slowly reemerged, although when depends on which food historian you listen to. Legend has it that Christopher Columbus took a stash of biscotti with him to the New World.

In the 1850s, a Tuscan baker named Antonio Mattei came up with a recipe for biscotti that won prizes at the exhibitions in Florence, London and Paris. His family jealously guards the secret for the biscuit they call "cantucci" in Tuscany.

Biscotti now has many regional variations, but generally people dunk it in espresso, coffee or a sweet dessert wine called vin santo. Over time, bakers began to add anise, almonds, amaretto, lemon and, as in the recipe below, cranberries and pistachios.

Cranberry Pistachio Biscotti
You can actually use any kind of dried fruit and nut in this recipe.

3/4 cup white sugar

1/4 cup butter, room temperature

2 teaspoons vanilla extract

1/2 teaspoon almond extract

2 large eggs, room temperature

1-3/4 cups all-purpose flour

1 teaspoon baking powder

1/4 teaspoon salt

1-1/2 cups pistachio nuts or walnuts

1/2 cup dried cranberries

In a bowl, whisk flour, baking powder and salt together. Set aside.

In a large bowl, beat the butter and sugar together until creamy, then beat in the eggs. Stir in almond extract.

Gradually add the flour mixture to the wet ingredients until incorporated.

Fold in cranberries and nuts by hand.

Refrigerate the dough for at least an hour or overnight.

Preheat oven to 325°.

Divide the dough into 2 equal pieces. If the dough is sticky, wet your hands with cool water to handle more easily.

Cover a baking sheet with parchment paper. Shape each half into a 12-inch-by-2-inch log, place on baking sheet and flatten slightly.

Bake until browned, from 20-25 minutes, depending on your oven. Remove from oven and cool for about 5 minutes.

When the logs are cool enough to handle, cut them into 1-inch thick slices. Put the slices on the baking sheet and toast in the oven for another 10-15 minutes, turning them once to toast each side.

Remove from the oven and cool on a wire rack.

5

TOZZETTI ROMANI

AKA LAZIO CHRISTMAS COOKIES

The gateway arch that welcomes visitors to Federal Hill is one of the most recognizable Providence landmarks. You can still hear Italian spoken on the hill, Providence's Little Italy. The neighborhood has a Columbus Theater, college housing, a piazza, Italian specialty shops and bakeries and Roman Catholic churches. Italian flags decorate the main thoroughfare, Atwells Avenue.

The neighborhood followed the typical Little Italy trajectory: A colonial neighborhood became a commercial district, then it got shabby. Then Irish immigrants filled its tenements during the famines of the mid-19th century. Then the Italians replaced the Irish. They came mostly from southern Italy—the regions of Molise, Campania, Lazio and Caserta.

Federal Hill enjoyed a heyday in the decade before World War II, when men gathered on street corners, and the sidewalks were alive with shoppers and children playing. Italian entrepreneurs ran their own shops. Italian grocers hung dead rabbits and lambs in the windows and displayed codfish in buckets.

After World War II, Providence emptied out. Nearly half the residents of Federal Hill moved to the suburbs. Efforts to revitalize Providence's Little Italy came to fruition with the election and reelection of Buddy Cianci as mayor. He often restaurant-hopped at the more than 20 Italian eateries that line a quarter-mile of Atwells Avenue—at least when he wasn't in prison. (There'd been a little unpleasantness with corruption.)

The most famous New Englander from Lazio is probably mob boss Raymond Patriarca. Patrarca presided over Providence's Little Italy and New England's mob from 1954 to 1984 in his nondescript Coin-O-Matic building on Atwells Avenue. He, too, went to prison.

Most Italian Americans from Providence found success the honest way. John Pastore, whose parents immigrated from Basilicata, became the first Italian American elected to the U.S. Senate in 1950. He also served as Rhode Island's governor. Others followed: John Anthony Notte, Jr., Philip Noel, Christopher Del Sesto and Donald Carcieri. Gina Raimondo, granddaughter of Italian immigrants, was appointed U.S. secretary of Commerce in 2021.

Tozzetti Romani

If biscotti is cantucci in Tuscany, it's tozzetti in Lazio, made with Lazio's excellent hazelnuts. "Romani" comes from the capital of Lazio, aka Rome.

1 Tablespoon baking powder

1/4 teaspoon kosher salt

1-3/4 cups all-purpose flour plus more for work surface

3/4 cup sugar

1/4 cup (1/2 stick) unsalted butter, room temperature

2 large eggs

1-1/4 cups hazelnuts

Preheat oven to 300°.

Spread hazelnuts on a baking sheet and toast for 10 minutes or when the skins start to split. While still warm, put them inside a clean tea towel and roll them around with your hands to remove the skins. Take them out of the towel and chop into large and irregular pieces.

In a medium bowl, whisk together baking powder, salt and flour. Set aside.

In another bowl, beat sugar and butter with an electric mixer until creamy, about 2 minutes.

Add eggs one at a time. Beat each one to blend, occasionally scraping sides of bowl, until combined.

Add dry ingredients, and mix on low speed to blend. Fold in hazelnuts.

Transfer dough to a lightly floured work surface and knead just to bring together, about twice. Form into a log about 14 inches long, 2 inches wide and 1 inch thick. Line a baking sheet with parchment and put log on it.

Raise oven temperature to 350°.

Bake about 25 minutes until golden and slightly firm. Transfer from baking sheet to a wire rack and let cool.

Using a serrated knife, slice log diagonally 1/2-inch thick. Arrange slices on same sheet; bake until golden brown, 15–20 minutes. Turn and bake until other side is golden brown, 5-10 minutes longer. Transfer from baking sheet to a wire rack. Let tozzetti cool.

Serve with sweet dessert wine; they're meant to be dunked.

6

Providence Knot Cookies

From Nonna's recipe box

Nearly one in five Rhode Islanders, 18.9 percent, claims Italian ancestry. That makes the Ocean State the most Italian in the country—except when Connecticut noses ahead. Rhode Island once had eight Italian newspapers and several Italian radio programs. Not to mention dozens and dozens of Italian bakeries.

How did Rhode Island get to be so Italian? It had textile mills, jewelry factories, foundries and construction firms that needed thousands of low-wage workers.

Italians started coming in waves around 1880. In 1870, twenty-seven people of Italian descent lived in Providence. That number multiplied sixfold over the next decade, then began to explode in 1880 when 1,519 immigrants, with 471 American-born children, lived in Providence alone.

On Columbus Day in 1910, Providence suddenly realized just how many Italians lived in the city. . Charles Carroll, a historian, described a parade in his book, *Rhode Island: Three Centuries of Democracy:* "For hours, Italian divisions poured through the city streets in rapid succession at steady military pace, unceasingly and apparently inexhaustively...Rhode Island had become conscious of its Italian population in a day."

By then, the Port of New York, where so many Italian immigrants arrived, had gotten terribly congested. Providence expanded its own port to accommodate transatlantic shipping. In 1911, the Fabre line, a French shipping company, began regular service between

Naples and Providence. In the 1920s, only two other East Coast ports—New York and Boston—received more immigrants than Providence.

In addition to Federal Hill, Italian immigrants moved to Eagle Park, the North End, Charles Street and Silver Lake. They also moved to Johnston, still the most Italian community in Rhode Island.

Italian immigrants identified more closely with their region or village than with the larger country. In America, they moved to neighborhoods where family and friends already lived: Families from Fornelli moved to the village of Natick in West Warwick. From Aliano, Raviscania and Sant' Angelo D'Alife they went to West Barrington. From Calabria, Cocenza and especially Acri they settled in Westerly. From Itri they moved to Knightsville in Cranston.

Italian women handled the finances, taught the children and cooked the food. For special occasions they would make sweets, like these Italian knot cookies. They're also known as unicetti, taralli dolci and anginetti.

Providence Knot Cookies

This recipe was adapted from one handed down through generations of one Providence Italian family. It makes a huge amount of cookies, but an Italian household needed a lot for visiting friends and relatives.

For the dough

6 cups all-purpose flour

6 large eggs at room temperature

1/2 pound butter

2 cups sugar

1-1/2 Tablespoons baking powder

1 Tablespoon vanilla

1 Tablespoons almond extract (or anise)

For the glaze

1 cup powdered sugar

Milk as needed

1 dash almond extract

Jimmies or colored sugar, for an extra festive touch

To make the cookies

Cream butter and sugar.

Beat in eggs, baking powder, extracts and half the flour.

Add remaining flour until a stiff dough forms.

Form dough into a ball, wrap in plastic and refrigerate for at least an hour.

Preheat oven to 350°.

Tear off pieces of the dough and roll into 1-1/2-inch balls.

Roll out each ball of dough into 4-inch logs. Form into knots.

Line a baking sheet with parchment paper and bake for 13-15 minutes. Let cool.

To make the glaze

In a bowl, put powdered sugar. Add the extract (just a splash) and a little milk.

Continue to add milk until it gets smooth. It should ribbon when it drips off the spoon.

Once cookies are cooled, dip the tops of each one into the glaze, or drizzle glaze over the cookies, and let dry.

Top with colored sugar or jimmies.

7

BRUTTI MA BUONI

GLUTEN FREE!

These "ugly but good" (brutti ma buoni) cookies have been sold in bakeries all over Lazio since the 1800s. They're delicious, effortless and gluten free. Both Lombardy and Piedmont claim them—but again, with regional differences. In Prato they're made with almonds and flour.

You may find brutti ma buoni at the local bakeries in Cranston, Rhode Island, where the street-sign poles are painted red, white and green. Italian restaurants and bakeries line Cranston Street.

Much of Cranston's sizeable Italian-American population has ancestors from the Lazian city of Itri, halfway between Naples and Rome.

Cranston's Italians settled in the Knightsville neighborhood starting around 1900. They came to work in the factories and mills. Some farmed, some worked in the building trades and others set up their own shops.

The city has a weeklong St. Mary's Feast in July, modeled on the Feast of the Madonna della Civita, which Itri celebrates.

During the festa, men carry a statue of the Madonna through the streets, while others follow carrying candles and praying. The Madonna can rest on tables along the parade route. Flower petals are scattered at her feet and dollar bills pinned to her robe.

Brutti ma Buoni

There are many different versions of Brutti ma Buoni all over Italy. Here is a Lazian version.

1-1/2 cups raw hazelnuts
1-1/2 cups confectioners' sugar
Pinch of salt
1 large egg white, room temperature
2 teaspoons pure vanilla extract

Preheat the oven to 400°.

Spread the hazelnuts on a large baking sheet with a rim and toast for about 12 minutes. The nuts should smell good and the skins blister. Spread a clean kitchen towel on your work surface and transfer the nuts to it until they're cool. Rub them together to remove their skins (they don't have to be perfectly removed).

Put the hazelnuts, confectioners' sugar and salt in a food processor and pulse until finely chopped. Scrape the mixture into a medium bowl.

In a separate bowl, beat the egg white slightly. Stir into the hazelnut mixture and add vanilla.

Line the baking sheet with parchment paper. Using a Tablespoon, drop globs of the hazelnut dough onto the baking sheet about an inch apart.

Bake the cookies in the center of the oven for 13-15 minutes, until browned in spots. (About 13 minutes for chewy cookies and 15 minutes for crisper cookies.) Let them cool on the baking sheet before serving.

8

STRUFFOLI

LOOK FOR THEM ON THE CHRISTMAS TABLE

Y ou may think of Westerly, Rhode Island, as the home of Taylor Swift, but 30 percent of the population claims Italian ancestry. (And Taylor Swift is actually part Italian.)

The first Italians to arrive in Westerly came from Carrara in the 1870s and 1880s. Talented stonecutters, they came to work in the town's granite quarries. Rhode Island School of Design professor Stephen Macomber praised their craftsmanship.

"They bequeathed upon our town the best in Italian culture that stemmed from the Renaissance of centuries before, thus issuing a golden era in the granite arts that remains, perhaps, the chief glory of Westerly's past," Macomber wrote.

The Carraran stonecutters in Westerly were followed by Neapolitans, Abruzzese, Sicilians and especially Calabrians. They worked in the building trades, in textile mills, as farmers and as merchants.

Many, if not most, of the Italian Americans in Westerly came from one town in Calabria—Acri, which has 21,000 residents. The Church of the Immaculate Conception in Westerly celebrates the feast day of a Catholic saint from Acri, Sant'Angelo d'Acri.

Deep-fried, syrup-soaked honey balls make a special treat at Christmas in southern Italy. Calabrians call them pignolata, but Neapolitans call them struffoli. You'll often find them on an Italian table at Christmas!

Struffoli

Give yourself plenty of time to make all these marble-sized honey balls, and be sure to make them all the same size.

For the dough

4 cups all-purpose flour

1 Tablespoon sugar

Zest from one orange, or half an orange and half a lemon

1/4teaspoon salt

1/4 teaspoon cinnamon

4 large eggs

1 Tablespoon unsalted butter

1 teaspoon rum, grappa or vanilla

3 cups vegetable oil for frying

For the glaze

2 cups honey (make sure it's good quality)

1/2 cup sugar

1/3 cup water

1/4 cup jimmies

To make the cookies

In a bowl or food processor, mix the flour, sugar, salt and cinnamon.

In a separate bowl, beat the eggs lightly and add the rum (or grappa or vanilla).

Add butter to the dry ingredients and beat. Slowly add egg while beating. Add a Tablespoon of water, continuing to beat, and then the zest until combined. Remove from the bowl and form into a ball.

On a clean work surface, knead the dough for a few minutes, cover in plastic wrap and let rest in the refrigerator for an hour.

Put honey in large, wide saucepan, big enough to put all the balls in at once. Add sugar and water.

Remove dough from refrigerator. Cut off a piece, roll into a log about a half-inch thick and slice off pieces also a half-inch thick. Roll into balls.

Place paper towels on a baking sheet and heat the oil to 350° in a saucepan. Fry the balls in the oil until puffed and golden brown, about 2 minutes. Remove with a slotted spoon and place on paper towels.

To glaze the cookies

Have your serving platter ready. Bring the heat to low under the honey mixture until all the sugar is dissolved. Then boil for about 4 minutes, until the honey darkens slightly. Turn the heat off and add the balls, tossing with a wire skimmer until they are all coated. Fish them out, letting excess syrup drip back into the pan, and mound them on the serving platter like a pyramid. (Or you can form them into a wreath.) Let cool and sprinkle with jimmies.

(From The Italians in Rhode Island, The Age of Exploration to the Present, 1524-1989, by Carmela E. Santoro, published by The Rhode Island Heritage Commission and The Rhode Island Publications Society, Providence, 1990.)

9

CUCIDATI

A TREAT FROM THE CONVENT

In Italy, elaborate, time-consuming pastries were typically not made in home kitchens. Italians bought them for holidays or on the way home from church. They could get them at the pasticcieria or the convent.

Italian desserts, in fact, owe much to the cloistered nuns in monasteries during the Dark Ages. They had the time and equipment to make complex confections, which they sold to support themselves and the monks. Each monastery had its own specialty. The monastery of Martarona invented the technique of shaping marzipan into realistic looking fruits and vegetables. The monastery in Catania created Minni di virgini, St. Agatha's breasts, to honor the city's patron saint. The Benedictine convent of Palma di Montechiaro still makes cassatella and biscotti ricci del Gattopardo. Nuns even marketed cannoli—a phallic symbol—during Carnevale.

They sold their goodies through a small convent window, sometimes with bars on them. Though the monasteries guarded the secrets of their pastry specialty, nuns sometimes left and took the secret with them, then leaked them to their village.

Cucidati, or Italian fig cookies, are made with citrus, spices and figs characteristic of Southern Italian cooking. Now, in some Sicilian households, the elaborate preparation of cucidati marks the beginning of the festive Christmas season. Several family members (women of course) would be enlisted to make and roll the dough, mix the filling, cut the dough, assemble the cookies and then decorate them.

Cucidati

Give yourself plenty of time to make this southern Italian Christmas treat.

For the dough

1/2 cup unsalted butter, room temperature

1/4 cup sugar

1/4 cup light brown sugar

1 large egg, room temperature

1 teaspoon vanilla extract

1-3/4 cups all-purpose flour

1/4 teaspoon baking soda

1/2 teaspoon salt

For the filling

1 cup dried figs, stems removed and diced

1/4 cup chopped pitted dates, finely chopped

1/4 cup raisins

1/2 cup orange juice

1/2 cup diced candied orange peel

2 Tablespoons sugar

1 teaspoon lemon zest

1/4 teaspoon ground cinnamon

1/3 cup blanched almonds chopped fine

2 Tablespoons dark spiced rum or Grand Marnier orange liqueur (optional)

For the lemon glaze

1 cup powdered sugar, sifted

2 teaspoons fresh lemon juice (add more if needed)

Jimmies

To make the dough

Whisk together the flour, baking soda and salt. Set aside.

In a large bowl, beat the butter with an electric mixer until creamy. Mix in the white and brown sugar. Add the egg and vanilla, still mixing.

Scrape the sides of the bowl and beat again for a few seconds.

Slowly add the flour mixture to the dough, mixing on a low speed.

Divide the dough in half and form each half into a rectangle. Wrap it in plastic wrap and refrigerate for at least three hours or overnight.

To make the filling

In a small saucepan, combine the figs, dates, orange juice, candied orange peel, sugar, lemon zest and cinnamon. Bring the mixture to a boil over medium-high heat.

Reduce the heat to medium-low and simmer for 5 to 8 minutes, stirring occasionally, until fruit is soft and the mixture is thick. Remove from the heat and add the chopped blanched almonds and 2 Tablespoons liquor, if using. Set aside to cool to room temperature. Cover with plastic wrap once cooled until needed.

Assembling the cookies

Preheat oven to 375°. Line a baking sheet with parchment paper. Take the dough from the refrigerator and let it rest for 15 minutes.

Put wax or parchment paper (at least 14-by-10 inches) on a clean work surface and dust with flour. Roll half the dough into a 10-by-8-inch rectangle. Cut each rectangle into two 10-by-4-inch strips. Put 1/4 of the filling down the center of each strip in a rounded mound. Take the sides of the paper and use it to take the dough and filling into the refrigerator for 10-15 minutes.

Take the dough out of the refrigerator. Using the parchment paper, lift one long side of the dough up and over the filling. Repeat with the opposite side to form a tube and enclose the filling. The dough should overlap slightly. Pinch the edges closed.

Put the filled strips onto the baking sheet, seam side down. Bake for 11-13 minutes or until lightly browned.

Remove from the oven and, with a large, thin knife, slice each strip diagonally into 1-inch pieces. Transfer the cookies to a wire rack to cool.

To make the glaze

In a small bowl, combine the powdered sugar and lemon juice and whisk until smooth. Drizzle on each cookie, then top with jimmies.

10

LEMON RICOTTA COOKIES

WITH THANKS TO THE ARAB CONQUERORS

Sicily, an island in the Mediterranean, has many fishing ports, and fish of all kinds are especially important to Sicilian cuisine. So are citrus fruits—limoncello is Sicilian—and ricotta, an essential ingredient to Sicily's most famous treat, the cannoli.

The first Sicilian fishermen arrived in Boston around 1890. Nearly all were poor and unable to speak English. Most came from Sciacca, and they brought with them the town's annual feast in honor of Madonna del Soccorso. Though the fleet is now gone, the festa is still celebrated in Boston's North End in August as the Fisherman's Feast.

In the beginning, Sicilian dory hook-fishermen rowed and sailed little wooden boats to fish in Boston Harbor alongside Yankee schooners. By 1908, a Sicilian fisherman bought the first motor fishing boat, and others soon followed. Eventually the so-called "guinea fleet" expanded to Gloucester, Massachusetts.

In 1909, a newspaper reporter interviewed Frank Ragusa, an Italian fisherman who had financially backed much of the fleet. The *Out of Gloucester* blog quoted the interview:

"The Italians are very hardworking, industrious men. I don't know of any class who work harder," Ragusa said. "They are up early and late, and they go out in all kinds of weather, winter and summer. Some of them start for the fishing grounds at midnight, others at 1 o'clock, others at 2, and so on."

Lemons, by the way, came to Sicily from North Africa. Arab conquerors began to plant citrus groves in Sicily around 850.

Lemon Ricotta Cookies

Lemon Ricotta cookies would have been a nice Christmas treat for those hardworking fishermen. They're also easy to make.

For the dough

2-1/2 cups all-purpose flour

1 teaspoon baking powder

1 teaspoon salt

1 stick unsalted butter, softened

2 cups sugar

2 large eggs, room temperature

1 (15-ounce) container whole milk ricotta cheese

3 Tablespoons lemon juice

Zest of one lemon

3 Tablespoons lemon juice

For the icing

1-1/2 cups powdered sugar

3 Tablespoons lemon juice

Zest of one lemon

To make the dough

In a medium bowl whisk together the flour, baking powder and salt. Set aside.

In a large bowl combine the butter and the sugar. Beat with an electric mixer until light and fluffy, 3 to 5 minutes. Add the egg, whisking until it is fully absorbed; then add the other, using the same technique. Add the ricotta cheese, lemon juice and lemon zest. Beat to combine. Slowly stir in the dry ingredients.

Make a ball with the dough, cover with plastic wrap and refrigerate for 1 hour.

Preheat oven to 375°. Line 2 baking sheets with parchment paper. Spoon about one Tablespoon of dough for each cookie onto the baking sheets. Bake for 15 minutes, until slightly golden at the edges. Remove from the oven and let the cookies cool on the baking sheet for 20 minutes.

To make the icing

In a small bowl, mix together the confectioner's sugar, lemon juice and lemon zest until smooth. Spoon the glaze onto each cookie or dip the top of the cookie into the glaze. Let the glaze harden for about 2 hours.

11

ANICINI

THE PERFECT END TO A GENOESE CHRISTMAS LUNCH

In Genoa, the bay tree symbolizes Christmas. Special candles illuminate the traditional Christmas lunch, which begins with natalini, special pasta in capon broth. The rich meal ends with pandolce, the Genovese Christmas cake since the sixteenth century, and anicini, the signature Christmas cookie.

The Genoese were the first to arrive in Boston's North End, by then a crowded Irish and Jewish slum. Most came in the 1860s. They thought of themselves as Genoese, not Italian, as Genoa had only just unified with the Kingdom of Italy in 1861.

The Genoese immigrants, fewer than 200 of them, settled in a three-block area next to a slaughterhouse. Those first Genoese sold produce, wine, cheese and olive oil from storefronts, pushcarts and Haymarket stalls. Luigi Pastene started out as a pushcart vendor after he arrived from Genoa in 1848. In 1874, he and his son started an import company, Pastene. His descendants still run the company from its headquarters in Canton, Massachusetts.

Anicini

Here's the recipe for that Genoese Christmas treat. You don't have to wait until after Christmas lunch to indulge.

10 Tablespoons butter

1 cup sugar

3 large eggs, room temperature

2-1/3 cups flour

2 Tablespoons baking powder

1 Tablespoon anise extract

Preheat oven to 350°.

In a medium bowl, whisk together the flour and baking powder. Set aside.

In a big bowl, beat the butter and the sugar together until soft and foamy.

Whisk in the eggs one by one and then stir in the anise extract.

Gradually add in the flour and the baking powder while mixing on a low speed.

On a clean, floured work surface, roll the dough out into a sheet, about 1-1/2 inches thick.

Line a baking sheet with parchment paper. Place the loaf on the baking sheet and bake for 20 minutes.

Remove from the oven, then use a serrated knife to cut into 1-inch slices.

Return them to the oven and bake for 10-15 minutes more or until they are golden brown. Turn them once to bake each side evenly.

Remove from the oven and cool on a wire rack.

12

MOSTACCIOLI

HAVE IT YOUR WAY

After the Genoese arrived in Boston, more and more Italians followed: from Campania, Naples, Sicily, Avellino and Abruzzo. Each group settled in a section of the North End with people from the same village or province. Each neighborhood had its own subculture.

The newcomers from Italy also moved to East Boston and the South and West Ends. But most lived in the historic North End, where patriots had sacked Thomas Hutchinson's mansion and Paul Revere had taken off on his ride.

By 1900, 14,000 Italians lived in the North End. A nineteenth-century journalist and historian, Samuel Adams Drake, gives an idea of the poverty and discrimination the Italians faced. He described the North End in withering terms: "Nowhere in Boston has Father Time wrought such ruthless changes, as in this highly respectable quarter, now swarming with Italians in every dirty nook and corner. In truth, it is hard to believe the evidence of our own senses, though the fumes of garlic are sufficiently convincing. Past and present confront each other here with a stare of blank amazement, in the humble Revere homestead, on one side, and the pretentious Hotel Italy on the other; nor do those among us, who [know] something of its vanished prestige, feel at all at home in a place where our own mother-tongue no longer serves us."

Drake would have been oblivious to the differences in subcultures among the different people of the North End. Those differences show up in mostaccioli cookies, which a cook named Bartolomeo Scappi served at a lunch for his boss, Pope Pius V, in the sixteenth century.

Most mostaccioli use a grape syrup called must, or mosto cotto. Except in Puglia, where they use cooked figs. Mostaccioli usually don't have anise, except in Avigliano. They're usually rhomboid or diamond, except in Calabria, where they're called 'nzuddha and shaped like animals, flowers and fish. In Salento, they're called mustazzoli.

Mostaccioli

This is just one of many versions: If you can't find mosto cotto, you can substitute grape jelly, but it won't taste quite the same.

5-1/2 cups all-purpose flour

3 Tablespoons baking powder

1/2 cup unsweetened cocoa powder

3/4 teaspoon cinnamon

1-1/2 cups almonds

3 large eggs, room temperature

1-1/3 cups sugar

1/3 cup honey

1/3 cup mosto cotto or grape jelly

1/4 cup extra virgin olive oil

1/3 cup cold coffee

Zest of 1 orange

23 ounces dark chocolate, 70 percent

To make the cookies

Preheat the oven to 350°.

Scatter the almonds on a baking sheet and toast in the oven for 7-8 minutes.

Remove from oven, allow to cool and chop fine.

Raise oven temperature to 400°.

In a large bowl, whisk together the flour, baking powder, cocoa powder, cinnamon, and almonds. Set aside.

In a separate bowl, beat the eggs.

To the eggs add the sugar, honey, mosto cotto, olive oil, coffee and orange zest, mixing until well combined.

Slowly add the flour mixture while continuing to mix until incorporated.

On a clean work surface, knead dough for a few minutes. Form a ball. Dust it with a little flour, then knead it with your hands for a few minutes. This will be a soft dough.

Separate a small piece of dough (about one large handful) and roll it into a ball.

Transfer to a floured surface and flatten with a rolling pin until it is about 1/4-1/2 inch thick

With a knife, cut the dough into 2-inch strips to form geometric shapes.

Line a baking sheet with parchment paper. Put the cookies on the baking sheet.

Bake for 5 minutes. The cookies will appear puffy and soft.

Remove from the oven and let the cookies cool completely on a wire rack.

To coat the cookies

Melt dark chocolate in a double boiler with a few drops of olive oil.

Have parchment paper ready for dipped cookies to cool. Using tongs or a spoon, dip the cookies in the chocolate and then place on parchment paper.

13

NEAPOLITAN COOKIES

ITALIAN PRIDE

In the 1920s, 37,000 Italians lived in Boston's North End. Life was hard. They suffered bigotry, poverty, exploitation and disease. Many Italian children died of respiratory illnesses from living in overcrowded housing.

They had begun arriving in waves around 1890 and encountered hostility from the start. In 1905, about 200 Italian men returned from a day's outing in Sharon Heights. They marched home from South Station behind a man carrying an Italian flag and one carrying an American flag. A motorman ran a trolley car through their parade, and a number of the paraders hopped on the trolley and attacked the motorman and conductor.

More trouble followed. The North End captured the world's attention with the murder trial and execution in 1927 of two anarchists, Nicola Sacco and Bartolomeo Vanzetti. Many believed the two had been railroaded because of their ethnicity and radical political beliefs. Protests over their treatment broke out on every continent but Antarctica.

Less well known is George Scigliano, a young lawyer and politician who advocated for Italian immigrants. His efforts helped stabilize the North End as an Italian community and instilled pride in Italian identity. Scigliano defied the Black Hand while serving on the Vigilance Committee, which helped police hunt down thugs who preyed on poor Italians. He insisted publicly that most Italians were honest and upright, contrary to the popular stereotype. After his election to the state Legislature in 1903 he got laws passed banning two institutions that cheated Italians: immigrant banks and the padrone, or labor broker, system. He also helped form the first Italian-American labor union.

Scigliano died in 1906, only 31, of a mysterious ailment. After his death, a political battle erupted over renaming North Square for him. The Italians lost the battle but they did get to name a park after their hero. As historian Stephen Puleo noted, the battle over the square "was the first major political battle that Italians had waged with any kind of consensus or unity." That newfound unity can be seen in cookies.

Italian-American bakeries invented the Neapolitan cookie with three colors of the Italian—not the Genoese or the Sicilian or the Tuscanian, but the Italian—flag. In Boston's North End, you can buy them in Mike's Pasty Shop, Modern Pastry, Anthony Bova & Sons or Parziale's.

Neapolitan Cookies

Here's a recipe for Neapolitan cookies adapted from pastry chef Stephen Collucci. You'll need three quarter-size (9-1/2-by-13 inch) sheet pans.

Cooking spray

1 cup sugar

1 8-ounce can almond paste

3 sticks unsalted butter at room temperature

4 large eggs, separated

1/4 cup milk

2 teaspoons almond extract

2 cups all-purpose flour

1/4 teaspoon red food coloring

1/4 teaspoon green food coloring

1/2 cup raspberry jam, divided

1-1/2 cups semisweet chocolate chips

To make the cookies

Preheat the oven to 325°.

Coat 3 quarter sheet pans with cooking spray, then line them with parchment paper.

Break the almond paste into 1-inch pieces. In a large bowl or stand mixer, combine the sugar, almond paste and 1 stick butter. Mix until smooth.

Add the remaining 2 sticks of butter and continue mixing until smooth, scraping down the sides of the bowl if necessary.

Slowly add the egg yolks, then the milk and almond extract. Mix until incorporated. Add the flour and slowly mix until incorporated. Set aside.

In a separate bowl, whip the egg whites until they form stiff peaks. Fold the whipped egg whites into the flour mixture to form a smooth batter.

Divide the batter equally among 3 bowls.

Stir the red food coloring into the first bowl of batter until evenly pink. Do the same with the green food coloring in the second bowl. Leave the third bowl alone.

Evenly spread the batter onto the sheet pans, keeping the batters separate. Bake, rotating halfway through, 10-12 minutes until a fork comes out clean. Let cool completely.

To assemble the cookies

Spread half the jam on top of the green cake. Carefully separate the uncolored layer from the parchment, then place the cake on top of the green layer.

Spread the rest of the jam on top of the undyed layer. Separate the pink cake from the parchment and place on top of the undyed layer.

Cover the cake with plastic wrap and put a clean sheet pan on top of it. Weigh it down with heavy plates or cans, and refrigerate for at least 4 hours or overnight.

Take the cake out of the refrigerator and remove the weight and plastic wrap.

Melt the chocolate.

Spread half the chocolate over the top of the cake and put it back in the refrigerator until it's set, about 30 minutes.

Take the cake out of the refrigerator when the chocolate on top is solid. Flip the cake onto a clean cutting board and remove the parchment. Melt the remaining chocolate again if it has cooled and spread evenly over the surface. Return to the refrigerator for another 30 minutes, or until chocolate is set.

Take the cake out of the refrigerator and trim into a neat rectangle. Cut the cake into 1-1/2-inch squares.

14

CHAMPAGNE COOKIES

NON-ALCOHOLIC, THOUGH

Today, Massachusetts ranks as the fourth most Italian state in the country behind New Jersey. Close to 14 percent of Massachusetts residents have Italian ancestry, with a half-million living in metropolitan Boston.

Massachusetts Italian Americans didn't all live in Boston's North End. They moved all over the state in search of jobs and more breathing space. Many migrated north to the cities of Saugus, Everett, Medford, Stoneham and Lynnfield. In Revere, 35.7 percent of residents claim Italian ancestry, making it the most Italian city in Massachusetts.

Italians also moved south of Boston, to Plymouth, East Bridgewater and Carver. And they moved west to Springfield's South End, to Shrewsbury Street in Worcester and to the mill towns of western Massachusetts—places like Dalton, Uxbridge and North Adams.

In 1958, Silvio Conti, the son of Italian immigrants, was elected to the U.S. Congress from Pittsfield, where he'd grown up in the working-class Italian neighborhood of Lakewood. Conti had worked in the GE plant in Pittsfield until the U.S. entered World War II. He served in the U.S. Navy, and then went to Boston College and Law School on the G.I. Bill.

Postwar prosperity and programs like the G.I. Bill brought money, respectability and even fame to the sons and daughters of Italian immigrants throughout the state. Poet John Ciardi was born in the North End, but moved to Medford when he was 5 years old. Artist Frank Stella came from Malden. Aerosmith's Joe Perry, whose mother is Italian, grew up in Hopedale. Angelo Leno moved his family to Andover, where son Jay grew up. The

Magliozzi brothers, who for years hosted Car Talk on public radio, grew up in Cambridge. Mike Eruzione, who captained the U.S. Olympic team that defeated the Russians in 1980, came from Winthrop.

Champagne cookies, like Neapolitans, are Italian-American inventions that signify cohesion and pride. They're sold in Boston-area bakeries, often colored pink and green, and usually covered in jimmies. They're also easier to make than Neapolitans. However, they don't have champagne in them.

Champagne Cookies

These are easier to make than Neapolitan cookies and are still pink, green and white.

1-1/4 cup unsalted butter, softened

1 cup confectioner's sugar

1 teaspoon almond extract

1 teaspoon vanilla extract

1 teaspoon salt

3 cups all-purpose flour

Red and green food coloring

Cooking spray

1/2 cup jimmies

In a large bowl, beat butter until creamy. Add confectioners' sugar and beat on low speed until fluffy, 2-3 more minutes. Add salt, vanilla extract and almond extract and beat until combined.

Remove the dough from the bowl and divide into three equal sections. Wipe down the bowl and put one section of dough back into it. Add three or four drops of red food dye and mix into the dough, adding more until it turns the color you want.

Form the pink dough into a ball and transfer to a clean work surface. Wipe down the bowl again and repeat the process with green food dye. Form into a ball and transfer to work surface. Form the undyed dough into a ball and transfer to work surface.

Roll each ball of dough into a rope about 2 feet long. Be gentle; if it breaks, patch it together.

Press the three ropes of dough together and roll gently to form a log. Cut log in half.

Pour all of the jimmies onto a baking sheet at least 12 inches long and spread out evenly. Spray the first log with cooking spray, then roll into the sprinkles, covering the whole log. Repeat with the second dough log .

Wrap the dough in plastic wrap and refrigerate overnight, or at least for an hour.

Preheat oven to 350°.

Line baking sheet with parchment paper. Slice 1/2-inch cookies from each of the logs and transfer to baking sheets lined with parchment paper, leaving 2 inches between each cookie.

Bake until bottom of cookies are golden brown, about 12-15 minutes. Leave on baking sheet for five minutes before transferring to a rack to cool

15

PIZZELLES

ROUND, FLAT AND SMALL

Pizzelles may well be the oldest cookies in the world, as the ancient Greeks and Romans ate them. Two towns in the Abruzzo region claim to have invented the crispy waffle cookies, now a favorite at Christmas throughout Italy.

"Pizzelle" means "round," "flat" and "small" (think "little pizza"). The batter consists of sugar, eggs, flour, butter and flavoring—usually anise, but there are alternatives. The dough is pressed on a pizzelle iron, traditionally two metal plates embossed with a design, and then held over a fire.

In the early days of Christianity, pizzelles were imprinted with sacred images, such as the cross, and used as the Holy Eucharist during Mass. Families might custom-make their pizzelle irons with their family crest or meaningful symbols, and the irons were passed down through the generations. Today pizzelle irons are often electric and embossed with snowflake-like images.

Pizzelles are still soft when they come out of the iron, and they can be wrapped around a tube and filled to become cannoli. Or they can be shaped into a cone to hold gelato.

The tiny Abruzzese towns of Cocullo and Salle both claim to be the birthplace of the pizzelle.

The cookie plays a role in festas in each of the towns. Every May 1, Cocullo celebrates the Festival of the Snakes—_Festa dei Serpari_—to honor a Benedictine monk named San Domenico di Sora. In the eleventh century, snakes overran the village and fields, but San

Domenico got rid of them. During the festa, the townspeople cover his statue with many live snakes and carry them in a procession. Then they eat pizzelles.

Salle, about an hour away from Cocullo, claims the ancient cookie originated within its borders. Every June the town holds its own festival honoring Beato Roberto da Salle, a twelfth-century monk. People hang the pizzelles from trees and hold them during the procession as an offering. No snakes, though.

Pizzelles

If you don't' have a pizzelle iron, you can make pizzelles on a griddle. Drop the dough onto a hot griddle and put a griddle press on top of it until golden brown. Or, drop dollops of dough onto a greased baking sheet, press them gently with your fingers and bake for 8-10 minutes at 350°.

3 large eggs

3/4 cup granulated sugar

3/8 teaspoon salt

1 Tablespoon anise extract (or lemon or vanilla, if you prefer)

1-3/4 cups all-purpose flour

2 teaspoons baking powder

8 Tablespoons unsalted butter, melted

Confectioner's sugar or chocolate for topping

In a bowl, beat eggs and sugar with an electric mixer until light and fluffy. Stir in the melted butter and anise extract.

In a separate bowl, whisk together the flour, salt and baking powder. Gradually stir into the wet mixture. Dough will be sticky.

Preheat pizzelle iron. Brush with oil or spray with cooking oil. Drop batter by rounded Tablespoonfuls onto the iron. Close and cook until steam stops coming out of the iron, about a minute and a half, though times will vary. Remove and cool on a wire rack. Dust with confectioner's sugar or dip into melted chocolate. Store in an airtight container.

16

Caggionetti

The cookie of champions

In Abruzzo, caggionetti were once enjoyed after Mass on Christmas Eve and are now eaten during the entire Christmas season. To call them fried ravioli doesn't do them justice, as the filling includes a luscious mixture of chocolate, chestnuts, almonds, rum, lemon zest, cinnamon and honey.

They're made with the traditional Abruzzese ingredient mosto cotto—a concentrated grape syrup, or must, made by cooking the liquid from initial grape pressings.

The town of Ripa Teatina in Abruzzo is renowned for its vineyards and for its bronze statue of Rocky Marciano. He was the son of Pierino Marchegiano, who left Ripa Teatina in 1912 for Brockton, Massachusetts. Pierino married and had six children. His son Rocco Francis Marchegiano grew up in Brockton and became Rocky Marciano, the only undefeated heavyweight boxing champion and the model for Rocky Balboa of the Hollywood movies.

Pierino Marchegiano's journey was like that of many Italian immigrants who came to work in Brockton's shoe factories. His son, Rocky, followed him into the shoe factory, but he also dug ditches and laid railroad tracks. The Army drafted him in 1943, a time when Italian Americans were considered enemy aliens, though 1.5 million of them served in the armed forces during World War II.

Marciano began boxing in the Army and went professional when he got out. His career spanned a time when the Italian population peaked in Brockton, from 1947 to 1956.

Then, about one in four Brockton residents had an Italian surname or Italian heritage. But the "Brockton Bomber" wasn't just a hometown hero; he was a hero to many Italian Americans.

Caggionetti

Plan to make the filling a day ahead. Measurements are approximate. Grape jelly isn't an exact substitute for mosto cotto, which is expensive; the two have different flavors but grape jelly is as close as you'll get.

For the Filling

2-3 Tablespoons honey

1-1/2 cups toasted finely chopped almonds

2-1/2 cups chopped chestnuts

1/2 cup grape jelly or mosto cotto

1/2 cup candied peel

2 cups espresso

3/4 cups grated dark chocolate

Zest from 1 lemon

3 Tablespoons rum

2 teaspoons ground cinnamon

Oil for frying

Sugar and cinnamon to decorate

For the Dough

4 cups all-purpose flour

2 Tablespoons extra virgin olive oil

1 cup dry white wine

1 egg

1 pinch of salt

To make the filling

In a heavy pot, add honey and grape jelly or mosto cotto and stir on low heat until liquid.

Add cinnamon and chocolate and stir until chocolate is melted. Add toasted almonds, zest and candy peel and sugar, stirring, then add the chestnuts and mix well.

If it isn't thick and gooey, add more almonds and chestnuts. Cook on low heat, stirring, for another 2 minutes.

Take off stove and pour into a large bowl. Add rum and espresso. Mix well, cover and refrigerate overnight.

To make the dough

In a large bowl, whisk flour and salt together. Add the oil, egg and wine and, with your hands, slowly work it into a firm dough. Knead for about 3 minutes to make sure it's the right consistency. If it's too loose, add flour; if it's too dry, add water.

On a clean, lightly floured work surface, roll the dough to 1/8-inch thickness. Cut into 3-inch circles using a cookie cutter or a large drinking glass. Place 1 teaspoon of the filling onto the center of each cookie, fold over into a half circle, and pinch to seal.

In a frying pan, fry the cookies in 1-1/2 inch of hot oil. Don't let them brown, and don't put too many in at once.

When puffy and crisp, remove from the oil with a slotted spoon and drain on paper towels.

When cool, sprinkle with sugar and cinnamon.

17

SUGAR COOKIES

SIMPLY SWEET

Since 1922, people have been buying sugar cookies from Libby's Italian Pastry Shop in Wooster Square. Nearby, Lucibello's pastry shop has served up sweets since 1929. Italian restaurants line the streets, and locals argue about which is better: Frank Pepe's white clam apizza or Sally's.

Wooster Square is Little Italy in New Haven, the densest Italian-American city in the country. One in five New Haven residents has Italian ancestry, according to the U.S. Census in 2017.

The neighborhood was named after Revolutionary War general David Wooster because he owned a warehouse near Water Street. Before the harbor was filled, Wooster Square was close to the waterfront. Ship captains and wholesale grocers built large houses near the port. By the end of the nineteenth century, factories moved to Wooster Square, and so did Irish immigrants. The neighborhood went downhill.

Sargent Manufacturing, a hardware maker, moved into New Haven and brought workers from the Amalfi coast of Italy. More Italians followed, primarily from the Campania region. They made corsets at Strouse, Adler; boots at Candee Rubber Co.; clocks at the New Haven Clock Company; and carriage parts at C. Cowles. Many families opened small shops out of their homes.

Large tenement houses went up among the old mansions, and people started calling Wooster Square "Little Naples." In summertime you could hear opera and smell cooking aromas through open windows. Wooster Square had a macaroni factory, a bank, five bakeries, pastry shops, meat markets, a banana business and grocery stores that carried

Italian-language newspapers. Frank Pepe, who immigrated from Naples in 1909, famously started making his Neapolitan-style apizza in Wooster Square in 1925. Men played bocce and baseball in the park.

The neighborhood fell into poverty when factories closed during the Great Depression. The city planned to build a highway through Wooster Square during the 1950s and '60s, but preservationists rallied. Wooster Square was listed on the National Register of Historic Places in 1971 and has since gentrified.

In 1889, the Roman Catholic archdiocese bought St. Michael's, originally a Congregational church, to become an Italian nationality parish. Three years later, the New Haven Christopher Columbus Monument was unveiled in Wooster Square. Mayor Joseph Sargent gave a speech, saying, "May his statue serve to eliminate any differences between Italians and Americans." That wouldn't happen until after World War II. Then in 2020 Columbus was removed. But you can still buy Italian cookies in Wooster Square.

Sugar Cookies

Sure you can buy these in a bakery, but will your kitchen smell as good?

3/4 cup shortening

3/4 cup sugar

3 large eggs

1 teaspoon vanilla, anise or lemon extract

3 cups all-purpose flour

3 teaspoons baking powder

1/8 teaspoon salt

For the icing

1/4 cup milk

2 tablespoons butter, melted

1/2 teaspoon vanilla extract

2-1/2 cups confectioners' sugar

Food coloring

Coarse sugar or jimmies

To make the cookies

Preheat oven to 400°.

Whisk together flour, baking powder and salt. Set aside

In a large bowl, beat shortening and sugar until light and fluffy, about five minutes. Add one egg, whisking until it is fully absorbed; then add the others, one at a time, using the same technique.

Beat vanilla (or almond or lemon) extract.

Gradually add dry ingredients to creamed mixture and mix well.

Shape dough into 1-1/2-inch balls. Place an inch apart on ungreased baking sheets. Bake 8-10 minutes or until lightly browned. Remove to wire racks to cool.

To make the icing

In a small bowl, combine milk, butter, vanilla and confectioners' sugar until smooth. Tint with food coloring if desired.

Dip tops of cookies in icing; allow excess to drip off. Sprinkle with coarse sugar if desired. Place on waxed paper; let stand until set.

18

TARALLI AVIGLIANESE

AN ADDICTIVE SNACK

F rom just about anywhere in Waterbury, Conn., you can see the sixty-five-foot illu-
minated cross that changes colors according to the colors of the Roman Catholic
Liturgical calendar. It's a feature of Holy Land USA, a theme park founded by a success-
ful, devoutly Catholic lawyer whose parents immigrated from Avigliano. In fact, about
eighty percent of Italians in Greater Waterbury are Aviglianese, from the southern Italian
city of Avigliano in the province of Basilicata.

The lawyer, John Greco, founded the theme park because he wanted people to have
a place to reflect in peace. He built a chapel, the stations of the cross and replicas of
catacombs and Israelite villages. Thousands came to visit in the 1960s and '70s, but Greco
died. Without its founder, Holy Land USA wasn't maintained properly. Finally it closed,
only to be sold in 2013 to people who are trying slowly to bring it back.

Italians started coming around the end of the nineteenth century to work in Waterbury,
la citta dell'ontone (city of brass). By 1910, Waterbury was Connecticut's second most
Italian city with 9,000 Italians. Along Grand Street, pushcart peddlers sold watermelon,
fresh fish, olives and meats.

Ironically, Waterbury's most Italian neighborhood, Town Plot Hill, is marked not by a
giant cross but by a massive memorial to the Pilgrims. Just after the turn of the nineteenth
century, Italian families moved into the neighborhood, where building lots sold for $25.
They built their own homes, often in family clusters, and planted extensive vegetable
gardens. Our Lady of Mt. Carmel church and school went up in the 1940s and '50s, a

time of growing Italian pride and prosperity. Today, the four-day Italian festival at Our Lady of Mount Carmel Church attracts Italians of all backgrounds.

Greater Waterbury has three other Italian festivals: the largest, Festa di San Donato is held at the Pontelandolfo Community Club, covering twenty-four acres with rides, food, pavilions and soccer. La festa della Madonna della Libera is sponsored by the Cercemaggiore Community Club and attracts area Italians with roots in Cercemaggiore in the Campobasso province of the Molise region. Then there's the Italian street festival at the Sons of Italy in Southington.

Taralli is a ring cookie popular throughout Italy with the usual regional variations. In Basilicata, where it's especially popular, anisette is used, while other regions might use marsala wine.

Taralli Aviglianese

If you don't like the taste of anise, you can leave out the anise seeds and substitute a dry white wine for the anisette.

For the dough

6 eggs

1/2 cup honey

1/2 cup olive oil

Anise seeds (2 Tablespoons if you like anise, less if you don't)

2 Tablespoons anisette

6 cups of all-purpose flour

For the icing

2 cups confectioner's sugar

Water

Anisette to taste

To make the cookie

Put a large pot of water on the stove to boil. Preheat oven to 375°.

In a large bowl, whisk the eggs. Stir in the honey, olive oil and anise seed, then stir in the anisette.

Slowly add flour while continuing to stir.

Knead the dough until it forms a ball, not too compact and not too soft.

Cut off pieces of dough the size of golf balls. Roll them into ropes, make them into a ring and pinch the ends together. Drop them into the boiling water.

When the taralli rises from the water, they're ready. Let them drain on a towel for about 20 minutes

Grease a baking sheet. Place the taralli on it. Bake for about 20 minutes or until brown on top. Let cool.

To make the icing

Sift powdered sugar to remove clumps and measure 2 cups.

In a large bowl, add the water a Tablespoon at a time, gradually whisking until it reaches the consistency of a smooth icing. Whisk in a splash of anisette.

Using a spatula, ice the taralli.

19

Susamielli

S-S-Sesame

Many Italians came to America during the 20th century as earthquake refugees. Italy lies close to the fault line between the Eurasian and African tectonic plates, so it is vulnerable to quakes.

In 1908, a tremendous earthquake killed tens of thousands of people in Sicily and Calabria. In 1915, an earthquake took 30,000 lives -- 95 percent of the people who lived in Avezzano. Then in 1980, 3,000 died and 200,000 lost their homes in an earthquake with a magnitude of 6.9 in Avellino. The town of Pontelandolfo suffered badly under the quake.

Some of those homeless Avellinese fled to Connecticut. Many went to Waterbury. A number of Pontelandolfians moved to Bridgeport. Seven years after the earthquake 10 of those earthquake refugees met a cruel fate. They were construction workers on the L'Ambiance Plaza project when the structure collapsed on them, killing a total of 28 and injuring 22.

Two monuments to the victims were erected in Bridgeport.

Bridgeport is still one of Connecticut's more Italian cities, with 16.5 percent of its residents claiming Italian ancestry, according to the 2017 Census. Some will undoubtedly bring an old Campanian Christmas tradition to the table in the form of S-shaped Susumielli cookies. This version is made with Neapolitan pisto, the Italian equivalent of pumpkin spice, a holiday mixture of five or six different seasonings.

Susamielli

You'll need two scrapers to make this traditional cookie.

For the dough

4 cups honey

3/4 cup apricot jam

6-2/3 cups flour

1-1/8 cup sugar

4 cups chopped peeled almonds

1 teaspoon pisto

1 teaspoon ground cinnamon

1/2 tsp baking powder

1/2 tsp vanillin (not vanilla extract; you can find it in the baking section)

For the pisto

1 Tablespoon cinnamon (best Ceylon)

1 teaspoon white pepper, ground

1 teaspoon nutmeg ground

1/2 teaspoon ground cloves

1 teaspoon coriander

1 teaspoon star anise

To make the pisto

First make the pisto. Put anise (approximately 5 stars) and a teaspoon of coriander in a coffee grinder and chop into a fine powder. Then add the other spices and grind briefly to mix.

To make the cookies

Preheat oven to 350°.

In a large pot, bring the honey and sugar to a boil. Remove from heat and let cool for a few minutes. Then add the apricot jam to the mixture.

On a clean work surface, pour the flour and add the pisto, vanillin, cinnamon, baking powder and chopped almonds. Mix with the scrapers. Form a mound with the dry ingredients and make a well in the center. Pour the honey mixture into the well and fold in the flour using the scrapers until they form a homogenous mixture.

Let the dough rest for 10 minutes, and then cut it into regular pieces (about 20).

Flour the work surface. Roll each piece into a log, then shape it into an S.

Line a baking sheet with parchment paper. Place the cookies on the sheet. Brush lightly with water to smooth the surface. Bake for 10 minutes.

Let the cookies cool completely before storing them in sealed containers.

20

BEFANINI

EPIPHANY COOKIES FROM A GOOD WITCH

Befana is a good witch, ugly but kind, who brings presents and candy to good children and coal or a stick to the bad.

Her name may come from the Feast of the Epiphany (Festa dell'Epifania). Italian children expect her to bring them treats on the Feast of the Epiphany, January 6, at least if they're good. She rides from house to house on a broomstick, and she goes down the chimney.

Befana, a good housekeeper, will sweep the floor before she leaves. That symbolizes the way the problems of the year are swept away during the holiday season. The family usually leaves a small glass of wine and some food for her.

The story of Befana the witch varies. According to one legend, the Three Wise Men stopped by her house asking directions to the infant Jesus. She didn't have the answer, but she let them stay the night. The Magi then invited her to come with them, but she said she was too busy with her housework. Later she changed her mind and started to look for the baby. She's still looking. However, she gives presents to children because there is a Christ Child in every child. Many children also get a piece of rock candy colored black to represent coal because they've all misbehaved at least a little during the year.

In another version, La Befana was an ordinary woman who had a child she cherished. The child died, and the grief drove her mad. When she heard of the birth of Jesus, she went to see him and gave him gifts.

Many Italian families make befanini cookies on the eve of the Epiphany, marking the end of the festive holiday season. They're a Tuscan specialty, made with sugar, flour and butter, and decorated with colorful jimmies.

Befanini

Kids love these cookies, especially if you leave out the rum and double down on the jimmies. They're also easy to make.

4 cups all-purpose flour + more for dusting

2 cups unsalted butter, softened

1 cup sugar

1/4 cup whole milk

5 large eggs at room temperature

2 beaten egg yolks for egg wash

2 Tablespoons dark rum

1/2 Tablespoon lemon or orange zest

1/2 teaspoon baking powder

Pinch of kosher salt

Multicolored jimmies

In a bowl, mix the eggs and sugar into a froth.

Add the butter, flour, milk, baking powder, salt, lemon zest and rum. Mix until the ingredients form a smooth dough.

Let the dough rest in the refrigerator for an hour.

Preheat oven to 350°.

Roll out the dough with a floured rolling pin on a floured surface until it's about 1/3 inch thick. Use plenty of flour for dusting because the dough is sticky.

Use cookie cutters to form shapes. Place the cookies on a floured, buttered baking sheet or one lined with parchment paper.

Brush the cookies with the egg wash and sprinkle with jimmies.

Bake for 10-15 minutes or until golden brown. Keep an eye on the cookies to make sure they don't get too dark. Let them cool on a wire rack.

21

CANESTRELLI

NO YOLK, THESE ARE TASTY

Not all Italian immigrants moved into crowded city ghettoes. Poor Northern Italians moved to rural Matson Hill in South Glastonbury, Conn., where they planted orchards that somehow thrived in the rocky soil.

The Matson Hill Italians appeared in the 1911 Dillingham Commission Report, some 40 volumes that represented four years of work studying the impact of immigration on America. Two old-line WASP New Englanders, William Dillingham of Vermont and Henry Cabot Lodge of Massachusetts, wanted to keep out many of the new arrivals. Congress appointed them to chair the commission.

During their research, they visited the Italian orchardists in South Glastonbury and described what they found. "The Italians have taken the rough uncultivated land abandoned by the Americans, made it productive, and established a community that is well known throughout Connecticut," they wrote. The Matson Hill Italians created a "good" kind of foreign colony, the report said. They "are spoken of as being honest, hard working, and industrious. One merchant remarked that they were the best people to deal with. They pay their taxes before they are due and often meet the bank's demands with the same promptness."

The report noted that the South Glastonbury Italians faced a thick wall of prejudice. For years they tried to persuade the town to build a school in the district, but failed. "Finally one of the Italians donated the land on Matson Hill, where the present schoolhouse now stands, others contributed money to buy the necessary lumber, a few contributed their labor, and in this way a new schoolhouse was obtained."

Dillingham and Lodge eventually got their way, with a series of laws that kept out the "bad" immigrants while letting in the "good." The Immigration Act of 1917 restricted immigration from Asia and required all immigrants over 16 to pass a literacy tests.

Then the Immigration Act of 1924 began a national-origin quota system. It capped total annual immigration at 150,000 and created two classes of immigrants. The "good" immigrants faced much less stringent entry requirements than the "bad," who were limited by quotas.

Canestrelli, a crunchy kind of shortbread cookie, originally came from Monferrato in the Piedmont in Northern Italy. It has a characteristic flower shape with a hole in the middle.

Canestrelli

These cookies have an unusual ingredient: hard-boiled egg yolk. Be sure to have a flower-shaped cookie cutter on hand.

1 cup all-purpose flour

1/2 cup plus 1-1/2 tablespoons powdered sugar

1/4 teaspoon salt

3/4 cup plus 2 Tablespoons corn starch

2/3 cup cold unsalted butter cut into pieces

1/2 teaspoon vanilla

3 large eggs

Zest of 1/2 lemon

Place eggs in a pot, cover with cold water and bring to a rolling boil. Remove from heat and let sit 8-10 minutes. Run cold water over them. When cool, remove shell, separate the white from yolk and mash just the yolk. Save the egg white for something else.

In a bowl, whisk together flour, sugar, salt, corn starch and zest. Put in a food processor and add cold butter and vanilla. Pulse a few times. Add egg yolks and pulse until almost completely mixed. Move to a floured work surface and knead gently until ingredients are combined.

Wrap in plastic wrap or parchment paper and refrigerate overnight or at least for an hour.

Preheat oven to 325°.

Line 2 baking sheets with parchment paper.

Remove dough from refrigerator and divide in half. On a lightly floured surface, roll out a half of the dough until it's about 1/2-inch thick. Cut out cookies with a small- to medium-size flower cookie cutter and cut a hole in the middle of each flower with a straw. Place cookies on prepared baking sheets and bake for 12-14 minutes. Cookies should not brown. Let cookies rest 5 minutes on baking sheets, then move to wire racks to cool. Dust with powdered sugar.

22

PIGNOLI

A SPECIAL NUT

Sicily has fallen under the rule of many foreign powers, including the Phoenician and Carthaginian, Greek, Roman, Arab and Spanish. Each brought their culinary traditions to the island, creating enormous variety in Sicilian cuisine. Greeks brought wheat, olives, grapes, almonds and pistachios. Arabs from North Africa brought citrus trees. Spanish conquerors brought cocoa and vegetables from the New World.

But the essential ingredient for pignoli, the pine nuts, have grown in Italy for 6,000 years. They come from the pine cones of the stone pine tree, one of the current symbols of Rome. The Via Appia is lined with stone pine trees, also known as umbrella trees. Roman soldiers carried pignoli nuts on their way to conquer Britain. They were a good choice: pignoli nuts are packed with protein, antioxidants and healthy fats.

Almond paste, a traditional Sicilian food, has found its way into many different cuisines. It is a combination of finely ground almonds and sugar pressed together, sometimes with egg white, to make a paste the consistency of Play-Doh. Don't confuse it with marzipan, which has more sugar.

Pignoli cookies are chewy on the inside and crunchy on the outside. Made of sugar, egg whites and almond paste, they are rolled in pine nuts before baking. Since almond paste and pine nuts are both expensive, pignoli cookies are an extra special treat.

Pignoli

This is an easy pignoli nut cookie to make.

16 ounces almond paste

1-1/2 cups sugar

3 egg whites from large eggs

6 ounces pine nuts

Pinch of salt

Preheat oven to 350°.

Break the almond paste into 1-inch pieces and put it into the bowl of a food processor. Add the sugar and salt and pulse until combined, about 30 seconds. It should resemble corn meal.

Add 2/3 of the egg whites and process about 30 seconds. Slowly add what is needed from the remaining egg white until a dough is formed. The dough will be wet and sticky, but you will be able to roll it into balls between your hands.

Scoop out rounded tablespoons of dough and roll into 1-inch balls.

Roll the balls in the pine nuts. The stickiness of the dough will help the nuts adhere

Line a baking sheet with parchment paper. Place the cookies on the baking sheet 2 inches apart and bake until the nuts are starting to turn golden, about 15-18 minutes. Don't overbake.

23

TURDILLI

THE GNOCCHI-LIKE CHRISTMAS SWEET

Maine is one of the least Italian states in New England (along with Vermont), but nonetheless 50,000 people who claim Italian ancestry live within its borders. Their Italian ancestors began coming to Maine in the second half of the 19th century – to work as stonecutters in the coastal granite quarries, to build the state's railroad network or to put up paper mills and waterworks.

They began arriving in large numbers fromAbruzzi, Sicily, Sardinia, Apulia and Calabria around 1890. Many Italians collected their wages and returned to Italy. Some who stayed moved to rural towns like Hallowell, Pittsfield and Rumford. In 1910, the two most Italian places in Maine were Hallowell, a city with quarries, and Millinocket, a town with paper mills.

The Millinocket Italians came as bonded labor. They owed the padrone who brought them for their transportation to Maine. In 1887, 58 Italian laborers realized they'd been hired under false pretenses to work on the Canadian-Pacific Railway. They walked off the job and ended up at the almshouse in Bangor. In 1894, 600 Italians hired to work on the Wiscasset and Quebec Railroad were abandoned by their padrone. They went on relief in Waterville.

Some Italians moved to Portland's Little Italy on India Street -- as barbers, carpenters, fishermen, longshoremen, railroad workers and masons. They moved near the docks because that's where the jobs were. Giovanni Amato in 1902 claimed to have invented the Maine Italian sandwich for construction workers to take on the job. Amato's Italian delicatessen, now a chain, still sells the "Maine Italian" – a long bread roll with meat, cheese, pickles, peppers, onion, tomatoes and olives. (Virgilio's in Gloucester, Mass., claims its founder, Giuseppe Virgilia, "stuffed an assortment of Italian deli meats, a drizzle of olive oil and sprinkle of oregano inside their crusty four-point Italian roll creating our famous Saint Joseph sandwich.")

In Bangor, an Italian-Lebanese family ran a well-loved restaurant called Mama Baldacci's. The son of the owners, John Baldacci, became governor of Maine.

Eventually, Mama Baldacci's was torn down for a walk-in clinic. Portland's Italian Americans moved to the suburbs, and Portland's Little Italy is nearly gone. St. Peter's Parish, once the center of Italian life in Portland, is still active. Micucci Grocery Co., established in 1949, is still open on India Street, and so is an Amato's.

At Christmas time, Maine's Calabrian immigrants probably enjoyed turdilli, a deep-fried cookie coated in honey. Today you probably won't find it in any Maine bakeries; you'll have to make it at home.

Turdilli

You may want to cut this recipe in half, as it makes a lot of cookies. On the other hand, it *is* the holidays. A gnocchi board is useful for making the ridges, but you can do it with a fork as well.

12 large eggs, room temperature

1 cup olive oil

2 Tablespoons baking powder

2 Tablespoons Sambuca

1-1/2 cups sugar

6-3/4 cups all-purpose flour

3 quarts vegetable or canola oil

2 cups warm honey

In a large bowl, whisk together the flour and baking powder. Set aside.

In another, larger bowl, break the eggs and beat with an electric mixer. Add the olive oil and Sambuca and continue to beat. Then beat in the sugar.

Add 2 cups of the flour mixture to the wet ingredients. Mix together until smooth.

Keep adding the flour one cup at a time and beating. When the mixture gets quite thick, you may have to stir with a large wooden spoon. Keep mixing until the dough is smooth.

Dust a clean work surface with 1/4 cup of flour and turn dough onto it.

Knead dough until it is pliable. Form dough into a ball, put into a bowl, dust the top with flour and cover with plastic wrap. Refrigerate for at least 2 hours.

Set a large pot onto the stove. Put in 3 quarts of vegetable or canola oil. Turn the heat on high until the oil reaches 350°.

Meanwhile roll out pieces of dough into ropes about 3/4 of an inch thick.

Cut each rope into 1-inch pieces and make grooves into the pieces using a fork or a gnocchi board.

Test the oil with one piece of cookie dough. When it floats to the top and moves around, the oil is ready.

Put the turdilli into the oil, one by one.

It's important to put the right amount of turdilli into the pot; too many and they won't fry evenly, too few and they'll cook the outside too quickly, leaving the inside doughy. There should be a single layer that fills the surface of the oil with enough room that they can turn on their own.

Remove from the oil with a slotted spoon when they are golden brown, about 10 minutes for the first batch, about 6 minutes for the next batches. Let drain on a paper towel.

Turn the heat to medium-high after the first batch.

While still warm, put the turdilli in a large shallow dish and pour the honey over them. Toss them several times, making sure they're saturated. Store in an airtight container.

24

TORRONE

THE STIRRINGLY GOOD LOMBARDY TREAT

I talian food, tradition and language are tucked into the hillsides and small towns of Vermont. So don't be surprised when you open your Vermont Country Store catalog and see cucidati for sale.

In 1910, Barre had the largest Italian population in Vermont because of the granite workers who came to work in its quarries. Not only does the city still have an Italian grocery store, it has an Italian social club—Societa' di Mutuo Soccorso. The old Socialist Labor Hall is a museum, listed on the National Register of Historic Places. It used to have an Italian bakery attached to it.

The Vermont quarry owners couldn't keep up with the demand for carved stone, so they enticed Italian stonecutters to Barre with high wages. The stonecutters' art is on display at the town's Hope Cemetery, where workers carved their own headstones with images like angels, an 18-wheel truck. a soccer ball, Michelangelo's *Pieta* and a soldier smoking a cigarette.

Italians came to work in granite and marble quarries throughout Vermont. U.S. Sen. Patrick Leahy's ancestors, including his mother, were Italian. They came from Italy's granite and marble regions: Viggiù and Bisuschio in Lombardy and Carrara in Tuscany.

Castleton and Rutland, along with Barre, still have significant populations of people who claim Italian ancestry. One out of ten residents of Stamford, East Randolph, Bridgewater, Shaftsbury, Proctor and Graniteville claims an Italian ancestor.

Italians also came to Burlington's Little Italy to work on the railroads and in the lumber yards. Some worked as peddlers selling produce. There were Italian bakeries, Italian groceries and Italian restaurants. Today you can still play bocce in Burlington's Oakledge Park, as well as in Rutland and Grand Isle.

Vermonters were inspired by the slow food movement that began in Italy in the 1980s and started the first statewide slow food chapter in the United States.

Torrone, a Lombardic Christmas treat, is a slow and ancient nut and nougat bar. Give yourself at least an hour and a half to make it and plan to do a lot of stirring.

Torrone

You'll need wafer paper for this, two 8-by-10-inch pieces. It's not the same as rice paper. Look for it in the baking section of your grocery store.

2 sheets wafer paper

3 cups roasted almonds

1 cup roasted pistachios

1-1/3 cups honey (don't stint on quality)

1 cup plus 3 Tablespoons white sugar

2 large egg whites, at room temperature

1 pinch salt

1 Tablespoon lemon zest

1/4 teaspoon vanilla extract

Dried fruit (optional)

Line an 8-by-11-inch baking dish with plastic wrap, letting the ends hang over the sides. Place a sheet of wafer paper in the bottom.

Put almonds and pistachios in a warming oven (140°) so they'll mix in better at the end.

Pour honey into a heavy pot. Add sugar. Cook over low heat with a spatula, stirring constantly, until mixture turns from grainy to silky and smooth, about 30 minutes. Take pot off the heat.

In a medium bowl, add egg whites and salt. Beat until whites form soft peaks. Put the pot with the honey back on low heat. Gradually whisk 1/4 of the whipped egg white into honey mixture; then repeat process with three more batches of egg white.

Keep stirring over low heat until mixture turns a brighter white. It's ready after about 40 minutes, or when the mixture drips off the spatula and forms a ribbon that keeps its shape on the surface for 4 or 5 seconds. Or, you can add a few drops of the mixture to a small bowl of ice water; if it hardens enough to feel like soft clay it's ready.

Stir in lemon zest and vanilla. Add warm almonds, pistachios and dried fruit if you wish. Stir until it is evenly mixed.

Transfer torrone mixture to the prepared baking dish and smooth the top with a clean spatula (oiling it helps). Put the last sheet of wafer paper, shiny side up, on top. Lay plastic wrap on top of the wafer paper, gently pressing and smoothing for a flat top. Take the plastic wrap off the top.

Let sit at room temperature until cool and ready to cut, 1 or 2 hours.

Lift the edges of plastic wrap to take nougat out of the baking dish. Turn upside down and take off plastic wrap from the bottom. If it's hard to remove the plastic wrap, trim off the edges of the torrone first, then remove the plastic. Cut torrone into 1-inch squares.

25

ABOUT THE AUTHORS

Leslie and Dan Landrigan have published the New England Historical Society website since 2013. Both have won awards in their past careers as news reporters, which took them to every corner of New England. Dan saw witch trial mania while covering Salem, Mass., and followed the Jack Kerouac beat in Lowell, Mass. Leslie once got to hold the original Massachusetts Constitution (wearing gloves) while working at the Statehouse in Boston. They now live in Stonington, Maine, where they write books. This is their seventh.

Previous books include:

- *Eat Like a President: 30 Recipes from the White House to Your House*

- *Italian Christmas Cookies: And the stories of the Italians who brought them to New England*

- *21 Historic Thanksgiving Foods: 1615-1955*

- *29 Historic New England Apple Recipes: Apple Recipes from Yesteryear, 1615 to 1960*

- *New England's Hidden Past: 360 Overlooked, Underappreciated and Misunderstood Landmarks*

- *Bar Harbor Babylon: Murder, Misfortune and Scandal on Mount Desert Island*

45573072R00051